D1227760

1. F-18 Hornet No. 3, the carrier suitability test aircraft, during initial carrier trials aboard USS *America* on 3 November 1979. Hornets will replace the A-7 Corsairs and F-4 Phantoms of the US Navy and Marine Corps and will become those services' pre-eminent fighter/attack aircraft of the 1980s. (McDonnell Douglas)

WARBIRDS ILLUSTRATED No 34

US Naval and Marine Aircraft Today

DON LINN

ARMS AND ARMOUR PRESS

Introduction

Published in 1985 by Arms and Armour Press,
2–6 Hampstead High Street, London NW3 1QQ.

Distributed in the United States by
Sterling Publishing Co. Inc., 2 Park Avenue,
New York, N.Y. 10016.

© Arms and Armour Press Limited, 1985
All rights reserved. No part of this publication may
be reproduced, stored in a retrieval system, or
transmitted in any form by any means electrical,
mechanical or otherwise, without first seeking the
written permission of the copyright owner.

British Library Cataloguing in Publication Data:
Linn, Don
US naval and marine aircraft of today. – (Warbirds
illustrated; no. 34)
1. United States. *Navy* – Aviation   2. Airplanes,
Military – United States
I. Title   II. Series
623.74′6   VG93
ISBN 0-85368-730-7

Editing, design and artwork by Roger Chesneau.
Typesetting by Typesetters (Birmingham) Ltd.
Printed in Italy by Tipolitografia G. Canale
& C. S.p.A., Turin, in association with Keats
European Ltd.

The beginning of the 1980s heralded many changes in US naval aviation. The new (and often controversial) F-18 Hornet began its service career with first US Marine Corps and then US Navy fighter and attack squadrons. The new McDonnell Douglas-built AV-8B Harrier II, derived from the original BAe Harrier, entered squadron service with the USMC in 1984 and will eventually replace the thirty-year-old A-4 Skyhawk. New helicopters, too, are serving with the Fleet: Sikorsky's SH-60 Seahawk, the winner over Boeing Vertol's SH-61 in the Navy's LAMPS development programme, began Navy Operational Flight Evaluation at NAS North Island in early 1984. Conversely, the premier Navy fighter through the mid-1960s and into the 1970s, the McDonnell Douglas F-4 Phantom, finds retirement waiting by the end of the decade, and the LTV A-7 Corsair, the workhorse of the Navy's attack squadrons for nearly twenty years, is rapidly being replaced by the new F-18 Hornet. Even Navy Reserve squadrons are experiencing change, with the first F-14 and F-18 squadrons scheduled to form before the end of the 1980s.

Changing politics and advancing technology are also having an impact on naval aviation. The Reagan Administration, taking office in 1980, has increased military spending compared with the previous Carter Administration, much to the benefit of the US Navy and Marine Corps, whilst new electronics, radar systems and advances in computer technology have made aircraft systems more sophisticated and also more accurate. The 1980s are an exciting decade, full of changes. It is hoped that the photographs in this book illustrate those changes.

Don Linn

◀2
2. Replenishment of ships at sea is a job ideally suited to helicopters, as illustrated by this Sikorsky Sea King of HS-7 departing a US Navy frigate. Sea Kings have served with the US Navy since 1961 and will continue to serve into the 1990s, until replaced by the new Sikorsky SH-60 Seahawk. (Kirby Harrison/*Naval Aviation News*)

▲3

3. The first of eleven F/A-18 Hornet prototypes surrounded by McAir technicians prior to a April 1980 test flight from NAS Patuxent River. In 1982, after modifications to the nose area, this particular Hornet began new flight trials as the prototype RF-18 photo-reconnaissance Hornet at the McAir facility in St. Louis. (Author)

4. The third Hornet prototype, armed with AIM-9 Sidewinder AAMs, flies over USS *America* (CV-66) during sea trials in 1979. Initial firing tests of both AIM-9 Sidewinder and AIM-7 Sparrow missiles were conducted in 1981 from Patuxent River, and the trials over the Wallops Islands Test Range proved so successful that ground crews began applying 'drone kills', similar to Second World War fighter kill markings, to the Hornets involved. (US Navy)

5. In a demonstration of its weapons-carrying capability, Hornet No. 4 unloads nine 1,000lb bombs during a test flight from NAS Patuxent

▼4

River. In an early 1982 weapons trial one of the production Hornets took off from Patuxent River armed with four 1,000lb bombs, two each on the outboard wing pylons; three external fuel tanks, one on the centreline station and one each on the inboard wing pylons; a Laser Spot Tracker in place of the starboard side-mounted Sparrow missile and a FLIR pod in place of the left Sparrow; and a Sidewinder missile on each wing tip. The Hornet flew 1,240 miles non-stop, without aerial refuelling, to the Navy's Pine Castle target range in Florida and back to drop its four bombs. (McDonnell Douglas)

6. US Navy Test and Evaluation squadron VX-4 is responsible for the continual testing of F-18 Hornets and the aircraft's weapons systems. Based at NAS Point Mugu, California, VX-4 conducted the Navy Preliminary Evaluation (NPE) and Initial Operational Test and Evaluation (IOT&E) of the F-18 before its acceptance into the Fleet. (Tom Chee)

5▲   6▼

▲7

▲8 ▼9

7. A VX-4 Hornet, with hook down, comes in for an arrested landing aboard USS *Carl Vinson* (CVN-70) after an April 1984 training flight. During the Hornet's initial sea trials in October–November 1979, Navy test pilots made 32 arrested landings and catapult launches aboard *America*; the pilots reported that catapult launch characteristics were excellent. Throughout the sea trials the F-18 demonstrated 100 per cent aircraft availability, allowing testing to be carried out uninterrupted. (Author)

8. An early Full Scale Development Hornet armed with Sidewinder and Sparrow missiles during weapons tests conducted by VX-4 in 1980. Four FSD Hornets followed the original eleven prototypes, incorporating the modifications and design changes resulting from the prototype programme at Patuxent River and evaluating these changes before their implementation in production Hornets. (McAir/USN)

9. The first Hornet training squadron, VFA-125 'Rough Riders', deployed several of its Hornets to MCAS Yuma during January 1982 for weapons and tactics training. Officially formed on 13 November 1980 with a single F-18 borrowed from Patuxent River for the ceremonies, VFA-125 is home-based at NAS Lemoore, where the newly commissioned Hornet squadrons to follow will also be based. (Phillip Huston)

10. VFA-125 was first tasked with training instructor pilots who in turn will train the new F-18 pilots entering the Fleet. In this 1984 photo new Hornet pilots are completing carrier qualifications aboard *Carl Vinson*. Since its first carrier trials aboard *America*, the Hornet has successfully qualified on most of the US Navy's big aircraft carriers, easily adapting to the carrier environment and maintaining compatability with other aircraft systems. (Author)

11. The honour of becoming the first operational Hornet squadron belongs to VMFA-314 based at MCAS El Toro; in 1961 the 'Black Knights' of VMFA-314 were similarly honoured when they became the Marine Corps' first F-4B squadron. During the Vietnam War the squadron compiled an F-4B recored of 25,000 combat hours, and VMFA-314 continued to fly Phantoms until 7 January 1983 when the 'Black Knights' traded in their F-4Ss for new F-18s. (Author)

▲12

12. A pair of Hornets from VMFA-314 refuels from a Lockheed KC-130R Hercules tanker over the Pacific Missile Test Range during the squadron's first live firing of Sparrow and Sidewinder missiles in February 1983. The Hornet's first aerial refuelling took place over Patuxent River from a Douglas KA-3 Skywarrior tanker assigned to the Test Center, and since then Hornets have completed air-to-air refuellings from Grumman KA-6Ds, from the new McAir KC-10 and from the Navy's specially modified Convair 880 equipped with a drogue refuelling system. (Author)

13. Following VMFA-314 as the first operational Hornet squadron were two more Marine Corps squadrons, VMFA-531 and VMFA-323, both converting from F-4S Phantoms in 1983. Recently, however, Hornets have experienced stress cracks near the tail, causing a halt in deliveries to the Navy, Marines and Canadian Armed Forces. On 29 November 1984 McAir resumed deliveries after installing aluminium reinforcements at the base of the vertical tails on all F-18s. (Author)

14. A Tomcat of VF-84 during air operations aboard *Nimitz* (CVN-68) in the Atlantic Ocean during May 1982. The F-14 is the world's first operational air superiority fighter with a variable-sweep wing. Augmented by manoeuvring devices, the wing is automatically positioned for best lift performance throughout the flight envelope. The Tomcat's twin afterburning turbofan engines produce over 40,000lb of thrust. (D. F. Brown)

15. A 'Ghost Riders' VF-142 Tomcat on the flight line at NAS Oceana in October 1982, wearing an unusual mottled grey camouflage. In October 1968 the US Navy asked the aerospace industry for design and cost proposals for an all-weather air superiority fighter suited to Fleet operations. McDonnell, North American, General Dynamics, Lockheed and Grumman submitted proposals; early in 1969 Gruman won the competition with the design that was to become the F-14 Tomcat. (Author)

16. Although F-14s have never served in sustained combat, two Tomcats from VF-41 were responsible for shooting down two Russian-built Libyan Arab Air Force Su-22 fighter aircraft on 19 August 1981. One of these Tomcats is seen here on final approach to NAS Oceana in May 1982. Just visible below the canopy, and forward of the ejection seat warning triangle, is the black silhouette of an Su-22 applied by its crew as a reminder of that fateful day. (Author)

17. (Next spread) The striking squadron markings of this F-14 Tomcat readily identify it as belonging to the 'Sundowners' of VF-111, home based at NAS Miramar. The original Navy-Grumman contract signed in January 1968 for 48 Tomcats was valued at $806 million, which gave the first F-14s a flyaway cost of $8.5 million each, a substantial increase over the $4.62 million unit cost of the F-4J Phantom, the Navy's premier fighter at the time. (Author)

▼13

14▲

15▲   16▼

▲18   ▼19

20▲

18. In 1980, after the retirement of the US Navy's RA-5 Vigilantes, F-14s were fitted with a camera pod system mounted on the No. 5 Phoenix missile station, as illustrated by this aircraft from VF-124, adding photo-reconnaissance to the Tomcat's capabilities. The Navy-designed and -developed system proved invaluable for reconnaissance flights over Syrian positions during the US deployment to Beirut in 1983. Taking off from US aircraft carriers sailing off the Lebanese coast, the TARPS-equipped Tomcats were able to provide vital photographic intelligence for the military planners. (Author)

19. Two F-14s of VF-213 'Black Lions' on return to their home station at NAS Miramar, California. The normal F-14 take-off weight is 57,300lb, and a maximum of 66,200lb is reached in the Fleet Air Defense mission when the aircraft is carrying six Phoenix and four AIM-9L Sidewinder missiles and two external fuel tanks. The F-14A has a basic weight of 37,500lb, roughtly half-way between that of the F-4J and the F-111B. (Lt. R. M. Riley/USN)

20. A Tomcat of VF-101, the East Coast F-14 training squadron, landing on *Independence* (CV-62). A trainee pilot must carrier-qualify on both day and night operations prior to his assignment to a Fleet squadron, but before he reaches this point in his career he will already have spent more than two years in flight training, first learning how to fly the Beech T-34C and then graduating to jets in the Rockwell T-2C Buckeye and McDonnell Douglas TA-4J Skyhawk. (Author)

21. One of the oldest of the US Navy's fighter squadrons is VF-31, which converted from F-4 Phantoms to F-14 Tomcats in 1983. The squadron's famous 'Felix the Cat' insignia, first adopted in the late 1920s, has been carried on VF-31 aircraft from the Grumman SF-1 to today's F-14. During the Second World War VF-31, designated VF-3 at that time, produced two of the Navy's most famous 'aces' – Jimmy Thach, famous for developing the 'Thach Weave' manoeuvre in his Grumman F4F Wildcat against Japanese fighters, and Lt. Butch O'Hara, the Navy's first 'ace', who also flew the F4F. (Author)

21▼

▲22

22. An F-14 of VF-24 'Renegades' serving with CVW-9 aboard USS *Constellation* (CV-64) during operations in the South China Sea in 1980. At the outbreak of the Korean War in June 1950, VF-24 deployed aboard USS *Boxer* with their F4U Corsairs as part of Air Wing 2; during the course of the war VF-24 traded in their Corsairs for the new Grumman F9F-6 Cougar, ending the war aboard USS *Essex*. (Kramer/USN)

23. A Tomcat pilot at work in one of the most demanding jobs in the world. The aircraft is manned by a crew of two, the pilot and the radar intercept officer, the latter operating the AWG-9 weapons control system. This system is capable of detection ranges over 100 miles, track-while-scan coverage of numerous targets, multiple and simultaneous missile guidance, and 'look down/shoot down' at extremely small targets. (US Navy)

▼23

24▲

24. An underside view of an F-14 prior to launching an Advanced Medium-Range Air-to-Air Missile (AMRAAM) at the Pacific Missile Test Centre. The Tomcat's weapons-carrying capability includes six AIM-54 Phoenix, six AIM-7 Sparrow and four AIM-9 Sidewinder missiles, and a single M61-A1 Vulcan 20mm cannon. (US Navy)
25. An F-14 of VF-111 'Sundowners' coming in, hook down, for an arrested landing aboard USS *Kitty Hawk* (CV-63) following a July

1980 sortie. The size and shape of aircraft carriers may have changed over the years, but their mission is still the same – acting as floating airfields for Navy and Marine aircraft to defend the Fleet. During the last two decades the aircraft carrier has proved to be a valuable asset in the rapid deployment of American forces in reaction to political and military troublespots throughout the world. (US Navy)

25▼

▲26

26. Afterburners lit, an F-14 from VF-31 is catapulted down the flight deck of the carrier *John F. Kennedy* (CV-67). (Harrison/*Naval Aviation News*)

27. 'The Last of the Legend' was the motto adopted by VF-171, the Navy's last F-4 training squadron, before its 1 July 1984 decommissioning. Phantoms first entered Navy service in 1961, providing the backbone for Fleet defence for more than twenty years, until the introduction of the F-14 Tomcat. Now only the Marines operate Phantoms in front-line service, and these aircraft are due to be replaced by F-18 Hornets. (Author)

28. Two F-4S Phantoms lead an F-4J of VF-74 during an April 1982 training flight; the following year the squadron converted to F-14 Tomcats. The F-4S differs from the F-4J in having wing leading-edge slats, which have greatly improved the Phantom's handling characteristics and increased its turning capability. (Author)

29. The age of this F-4J of Navy Reserve squadron VF-301 (photographed in 1981) is reflected by the MiG-17 kill marking near its tail carried over from its Vietnam service. Navy Phantoms launched from aircraft carriers and shore-based Marine Corps Phantoms saw extensive combat service in Vietnam, often flying air strikes against North Vietnamese forces or acting in close air support of ground forces. (Tom Chee)

30. Based at NAS Miramar are two of the Navy Reserve's four F-4 squadrons; this VF-302 F-4J was photographed in 1981 wearing an early low-visibility camouflage scheme. Two of these Reserve squadrons have already begun their transition to F-14 Tomcats, and by 1986 the remaining two Phantom squadrons will convert to F-14s, thus ending 25 years of Phantom service in the US Navy. (Author)

▼27

▲31

31. The US Marines operate several F-4 squadrons, such as VMFA-312 (one of whose machines is depicted), but these are all expected to be replaced by new F-18 Hornets by 1988. By the time the last Marine Corps F-4 Phantom squadron converts to F-18 Hornets, Phantoms will have seen 27 years in Navy and Marine Corps service. (Author)

32. The only remaining RF-4B squadron is VMFP-3; an aircraft is seen here landing at NAS Fallon in 1982. RF-4B Phantoms first reached USMC squadrons in May 1965 and have served only with the Marines, the Navy utilizing the photo-reconnaisance capabilities of the RF-8 Crusader and RA-5C Vigilante instead. A photo-reconnaissance version of the F-18 will replace the RF-4B by 1989. (Author)

33. The most recent A-6 Intruder squadron to form is VA-55 at NAS Oceana during July 1984. VA-55, an A-4 Skyhawk squadron during the 1960s, is assigned to the new East Coast-based USS *Coral Sea* Air Wing, CVW-13. The all-grey camouflage scheme, typical of current

US Navy and Marine aircraft, is highlighted only by the darker grey 'AK' squadron tail codes and the winged seahorse on the rudder. (Author)

34. A VA-34 'Blue Blasters' A-6E on the flight line at NAS Oceana, home of Medium Attack Wing 1. Intruders are equipped with on-board digital attack and navigation computers that allow their crews to take off and fly to preselected targets at any altitude, including tree top height, deliver their ordnance and return to base without looking outside the cockpit and with no reliance on external navigation aids. (Author)

35. An A-6E Intruder of VA-34 sharing *Nimitz*'s flight deck with an A-7E of VA-82 during August 1982 air operations off the coast of Virginia. Intruders first entered squadron service with VA-42 'Green Pawns' on 7 February 1963 as replacements for Douglas Skyraiders, and after more than twenty years the basic design has changed very little from that of the first A-6A. (D. F. Brown)

▼32

33▲

34▲ 35▼

▲ 36

▲ 37   ▼ 38

36. An A-6E Intruder of VMA(AW)-533 (one of seven Marine Corps A-6 squadrons) on final approach to McGuire AFB after a 1981 training flight. US Navy A-6 aircrew training is conducted by VA-42 at NAS Oceana and VA-128 at NAS Whidbey Island; Marine Corps A-6 training is carried out by VMAT(AW)-202, known as 'Intruder College', at MCAS Cherry Point. (Author)
37. The chin turret on this Intruder of VA-36 identifies the aircraft as an A-6E TRAM (Target Recognition Attack Multisensor). This latest modification to the A-6 has increased its capability and comprises additional infra-red sensors, FLIR (Forward-Looking Infra-Red), video recording equipment and other electronics. Grumman's A-6 Intruder is one of the few true all-weather attack aircraft, joining company with the F-111, the Hawker Siddeley Buccaneer and the Panavia Tornado. (Author)
38. A January 1984 photograph of a VA-52 Intruder operating from USS *Kitty Hawk* and not yet wearing low-visibility camouflage. During the mid-1960s and throughout the 1970s, Intruders carried some of the most colourfully painted tails of Navy aircraft, but improvements in aircraft detection have resulted in a general movement towards drab grey low-visibility camouflage for the 1980s. (US Navy)

39. The Intruder tanker version, the KA-6D, is easily identified by the drogue chute housing located on the undersides between the airbrakes. The first production KA-6D made its maiden flight on 16 April 1970 with Grumman test pilot Chuck Sewell at the controls, a modified A-6A with a refuelling drogue having conducted flight trials as the prototype KA-6D during April and May 1966. Two KA-6Ds are usually assigned to each A-6 squadron. (Author)

40. The EA-6B Prowler is derived from the original A-6 Intruder and was designed for use in the Tactical Electronics Warfare role. A total production run of 32 EA-6B Prowlers, including four converted from A-6A airframes, has been undertaken by Grumman, delivery of the first aircraft taking place during May 1969 to VAQ-129 'Vikings' at NAS Whidbey Island and thus establishing the Prowler training squadron. (Tom Chee)

41. EA-6B Prowlers are operated by four crew members – a pilot, a navigator/electronics warfare officer and two electronics counter-measures warfare officers. Surveillance receivers in the pod-shaped antenna fairing atop the Prowler's vertical fin detect enemy radar signals at long ranges and feed the data into central digital computers in the aircraft; jammers are then automatically turned on to confuse the radars. (US Navy)

39▲

40▲   41▼

▲42

42. This underside view of an EA-6B shows the array of ECM pods used for electronic suppression and intelligence gathering. The Prowler combines high-powered jammers and sensitive receivers to disrupt radar and radio equipment of an enemy, its primary mission being to screen strike force carrier aircraft from acquisition and tracking associated with Soviet surface-to-air missiles. (Grumman)

43. A Prowler from VAQ-129, one of ten EA-6B squadrons, returns from a June 1984 training sortie; this example is devoid of ECM pods. The Prowler also functions to protect surface vessels from radar detection by interceptor aircraft, and from radar-directed cruise missiles. An improved-capability version of the EA-6B, tailored to react more quickly to increasingly varied threats, is under development. (Author)

▼43

44. The second US Navy squadron to convert from A-7 Corsairs to F-18 Hornets is VFA-25 'Fist of the Fleet', based at NAS Lemoore, California. The A-7 Corsair is admired for its endurance on long-range missions, but its pilots have often complained about the aeroplane's lack of speed in returning from a target, a problem which the F-18 will overcome. (Phillip Huston)

45. The US Marines have three Hornet squadrons based at MCAS El Toro. An F-18 from VMFA-531, the second unit to form at that base, is here preparing for a July 1984 training flight. MCAS El Toro is the Marine Corps West Coast F-18 base, and MCAS Beaufort will be 'home' for the East Coast F-18s. For the time being Marine F-18 pilot training is conducted by the Navy's VFA-125 at NAS Lemoore. (Phillip Huston)

 46

46. An F-14 Tomcat of VF-102 prepares to launch from the carrier *America* during a 1983 Mediterranean cruise. When the Tomcat was under development and undergoing flight trials in the early 1970s it received much criticism because of cost overruns, but these objections were settled and in 1982 the aircraft reached its tenth year of service. (Steve Daniels)

47. Flames shoot from the afterburners and condensation streams from the wing tips as an F-14 from VF-101 demonstrates the Tomcat's power and agility. VF-101, based at NAS Oceana, is responsible for East Coast F-14 aircrew training, as well as maintenance training for ground crews. (Author)

48. The final cruise for VF-171, the last F-4 squadron based at NAS Oceana, occurred on 27 April 1984; by June the squadron had been decomissioned. VF-171 was re-established in 1976 to take over F-4 Phantom pilot training from VF-101, that squadron turning its efforts to training F-14 pilots and ground crews. (Author)

49. An F-4S Phantom of VMFA-232 wearing the low-visibility camouflage adopted by both the Navy and the Marines in the early 1980s. The F-4S is the last version of the Phantom to be operated by these services. (Phillip Huston)

 47

▲50   ▼51

50. An A-6E of VA-85 photographed during an April 1980 flight from NAS Oceana. (Author)

51. Even the Prowler has not been able to escape the new low-visibility camouflage schemes adopted by the US Navy and Marines in 1981. Nevertheless, the EA-6B is a surprisingly easy aircraft to manoeuvre, even with external stores, and has adequate power with external loads, although Navy pilots report that the latter cause increased roll inertia when compared with the basic airframe. (Grumman)

52. A formation flight of aircraft assigned to the US Navy's Test Pilot School at NAS Patuxent River. Navy and Marine Corps graduates of the Naval Test Pilot School are assigned to one of the test directorates at the Naval Air Test Center, where they become involved in the test and evaluation of modern naval aircraft and systems. The Naval Test Pilot School was officially formed in 1958. (J. Harrison/*Naval Aviation News*)

53. A pair of A-7E Corsairs of VA-86 returns to the carrier *Nimitz*. During December 1963 Secretary of Defense Robert McNamara approved funding for a contract to LTV for the production of the then-new A-7A Corsair; this resulted from an earlier study by the Navy which looked for a replacement for the Douglas A-4 Skyhawk. The first A-7A was formally accepted by the Navy at Cecil Field, Jacksonville, Florida, on 14 October 1966. (US Navy)

54. An A-7E of VA-25 'Fist of the Fleet' a few weeks before the squadron completed its transition to F-18 Hornets in 1983. By the end of the decade, after serving for more than 24 years in the Navy, the A-7 Corsair's US military career will be limited to Air National Guard service. (Tom Chee)

52▲

53▲ 54▼

▲ 55   ▼ 56

55. A head-on view of two A-7Es of VA-27 with USS *John F. Kennedy* below. Although the A-7 can carry twice the bomb load of the Second World War B-17 bomber, its lack of speed in today's world of high-performance jet fighters is a liability. Initially the US Navy's acquisition of Corsairs included a Marine Corps requirement, but the Marines decided against the purchase of the A-7, opting instead for the new Hawker Siddeley AV-8 Harrier several years later. (US Navy)

56. Several A-7s are assigned to the Naval Air Test Center as NAS Patuxent River for the testing of new aircraft systems. Corsairs first arrived at the Center in 1965 during the aircraft's Initial Test and Operational Evaluation (IT&OE), before entering Fleet service. Since that time, Corsairs have undergone several design modifications, from A-7A through to the current A-7E and including the two-seat TA-7C trainer. (Author)

57. VA-303 is scheduled to become the US Navy's first Reserve F-18 Hornet squadron following transition in 1985; four reserve squadrons are currently equipped with Corsairs, and will in time similarly convert, serving with Reserve Air Wing 20 or 30, which are identified by their respective tailcodes 'AF' or 'ND'. Through the years the Navy Reserve has predominantly operated A-7A and A-7Bs, until recently upgrading to A-7Es. (Tom Chee)

58. A TA-7C two-seat trainer version of the Corsair serving with the East Coast A-7 training squadron VA-174, based at NAS Jacksonville. The TA-7C began as a private venture by LTV, but the US Navy funded $4.9 million for the conversion of 40 A-7Bs and 41 A-7Cs to the trainer configuration. Performance specifications for the TA-7C are similar to those of the single-seat A-7E. (Author)

▲59

▲60 ▼61

59. With its wing raised as an airbrake, this VFP-306 RF-8G Crusader prepares to land at Andrews AFB, its home station, following a photo-recce sortie. On 1 October 1984 this squadron was decommissioned. The RF-8, initially designated F8U-1P, made its first flight on 17 December 1957, and a production run of 144 photo-reconnaissance Crusaders followed. After modification, including a new navigation system and improved cameras, the F8U-1P changed its designation to RF-8G. (Author)

60. With the decommissioning of VFP-306, the bulk of the Navy's photographic reconnaissance is now undertaken by VFP-206, also home-based at Andrews AFB. F8U Crusaders first entered US Navy service on 28 December 1956 and served extensively during the Vietnam War, compiling an enviable combat record. Following nearly thirty years of service, these RF-8Gs of VFP-206 represent the end of the Crusader era. (Author)

61. The US Marines and Marine Reserves are the biggest users of McDonnell Douglas A-4 Skyhawks. Here an A-4E Skyhawk of Marine Reserve squadron VMA-131 returns to NAS Willow Grove

following a 1981 training flight. A-4s served gallantly with both the Navy and Marine Corps during the Vietnam War, only to be replaced by LTV's A-7 Corsair during the mid-1960s. Today only a few A-4s remain with the US Navy, primarily in the training role. (Author)

62. A two-seat TA-4J Skyhawk of Navy Reserve squadron VC-12 based at NAS Oceana. VC-12 flies both TA-4J and A-4E Skyhawks in various roles, which include acting as target tugs and as 'Aggressors' for air combat training. The A-4 is known by many terms of endearment, including 'Scooter' and 'Heinemann's Hot Rod' (the latter after Ed Heineman, the A-4's designer), but 'Skyhawk' remains the A-4's official name – a straightforward reference to its diminutive size and exceptional manoeuvrability. (Bill Cline)

63. Another version of the Skyhawk is the OA-4M, which is employed by the Marines as a forward air controller. It is a modification of the TA-4J which incorporates the ECM hump aft of the cockpit and a raised tail with an ECM antenna. The OA-4M is the last version of the two-seat Skyhawk; the first, the TA-4F, took off for its maiden flight during April 1966. (Author)

64. The last version of the Skyhawk to be produced by McDonnell Douglas was the A-4M, the final example of which is seen here in the markings of NAS Patuxent River. Photographed on 17 June 1984, this A-4M, serial number 160264, was the 2,960th A-4 to be built when it rolled off the McDonnell Douglas line in 1979. A-4Ms are readily distinguishable from other versions of the Skyhawk by the larger canopy, which appears almost bulged when compared to that of the A-4E. (Author)

64 ▶

◄65
65. Although nearly twenty years old, Marine Corps A-4 training squadron VMAT-102, based at MCAS Cherry Point, still utilizes the TA-4F Skyhawk in its pilot training programme, the first TA-4Fs having been delivered to Skyhawk training squadron VA-125 at NAS Lemoore on 19 May 1966. In converting the single-seat Skyhawk to the two-seat TA-4F the overall length of the aircraft was increased by 28in and resulted in a reduction in internal fuel capacity. (Tom Chee)

▲ 66

66. Student fighter pilots learn their craft in TA-4J Skyhawks assigned to the training command. Following Primary and Intermediate Flight Training in the turbo-powered Beech T-34C while assigned to Training Wing 5 at NAS Whiting Field, student pilots move up to the TA-4J Skyhawks for Advanced Flight Training; following graduation from Advanced Flight Training, they are assigned to Fleet fighter or attack training squadrons. (Author)

▼ 67

67. The most important flying skill that Navy and Marine fighter pilots must master is carrier landing, as demonstrated by this student pilot landing his TA-4J of VT-21 aboard USS *Carl Vinson.* Understandably, the emphasis on carrier-compatible skills continues all through the flying careers of Navy and Marine aviators, and pilots must continually requalify in day and night carrier landings and take-offs to maintain their proficiency. (Author)

68. A British Aerospace-built AV-8A Harrier of Marine Corps attack squadron VMA-231. Harriers have served with the Marines since 1971, but Marine Corps interest in the Harrier's V/STOL capability began in 1968 with two Marine aviators visiting Hawker Siddeley during the Farnborough Air Show. Initially the Marine Corps received approval to purchase twelve AV-8A Harriers, and this number eventually grew to 110, including eight two-seat trainers. Unlike previous US practice the total USMC procurement was built in Britain, the last Harrier being delivered in 1976. (Author)

69. AV-8C Harriers are modified A-model Harriers with added lift improvement devices (LIDs), which give the aircraft increased performance. Whilst waiting for the new McDonnell Douglas-built AV-8B Harrier II to enter service in 1984, the remaining AV-8As

began a retrofit programme utilizing improvements designed for the new AV-8B. The modified AV-8C began flight evaluation at Patuxent River in late 1982, the first being accepted into squadron service in 1983. (Author)

70. The Harrier II prototype during 1981 flight trials at NAS Patuxent River. The YAV-8B utilized the AV-8A airframe but showed modified intakes and double rows of auxiliary inlet doors surrounding them, lift improvement devices, and a new and larger composite wing. After nearly two years of evaluation, several design changes have occurred; externally, the most prominent of these are the revised inlet doors, a larger, single row having been found to be more efficient. (Author)

▲71

71. McAir technicians prepare the No. 3 FSD AV-8B Harrier II for another test flight. Four FSD AV-8Bs began flight trials at Patuxent River in 1983, each appearing in a different camouflage in an effort to determine the most practical scheme. (Author)

72. The first production AV-8B Harrier IIs were delivered to the Marine Corps Harrier training squadron, VMAT-203, at MCAS Cherry Point during the spring of 1984; initially, the machines will be used to train new Harrier pilots, as well as to provide transition training for AV-8A pilots. (Author)

73. The two-seat TAV-8A Harrier trainer of VMAT-203 is similar to the RAF's Harrier T.4. Eight two-seaters were ordered in 1973 and delivered during the summer of that year, when the first TAV-8 became operational with VMAT-203 at Cherry Point. The Marines have a dual mission for the TAV-8A: in addition to its role as a training aircraft, it is also capable of operating as an Airborne Tactical Air Controller, utilizing its full range of tactical UHF and VHF radio equipment. (Author)

▼72

▲74

74. S-3 Vikings replaced the ageing piston-engined Grumman S-2 Tracker in the anti-submarine warfare (ASW) role during the 1970s and will continue to serve through to the 1990s. The first of eight test and evaluation examples of the Lockheed built S-3 was rolled out on 8 November 1972 and began its flight test programme the following January. Initial Navy requirements called for a Lockheed production run of 191 machines. (Author)

75. A pair of S-3A Vikings of VS-22 armed with pylon-mounted 500lb bombs and photographed during a patrol from USS *Saratoga* (CV-60). Vikings can search, track and destroy the most up-to-date deep-cruising nuclear submarines with an impressive array of weaponry. The two underwing racks and the double fuselage bomb bay can hold 70mm or 127mm rocket launchers, flare dispensers, 1,000lb mines or conventional or nuclear depth charges. (Lockheed)

▼75

76▲

76. A Viking from VX-1 takes off from NAS Patuxent River, 1983. VX-1 was formed during the Second World War to develop new ASW equipment and tactics. The Viking's size and performance make it suitable for roles other than ASW, and Lockheed has converted two standard S-3As, one to a COD (carrier on-board delivery) version and the other to an airborne tanker, for continued evaluation to expand the Viking's capabilities. (Author)

77. The Anti-Submarine Warfare Directorate at NAS Patuxent River is responsible for evaluating new ASW systems, and while the S-3 was assigned to the ASW Directorate, and before its acceptance for Fleet service, its complete ASW capability was tested there. One of the Viking's major assets for its ASW mission are the various on-board computer systems used for tracking and identifying submarines, but these same computers can easily be adapted to perform other roles such as coastal patrol and fishery, pollution and smuggling control, thus taking full advantage of the S-3's technology. (Author)

77▼

78. A Viking on the 'cat' aboard *John F. Kennedy*, waiting for the signal to launch from the deck officer. When the catapult is fired the S-3A accelerates from zero to 120kts in 2.2 seconds. To meet its maximum specifications on launch, the Viking must be able to withstand peak catapult forces equal to 5g; likewise, carrier-arrested landings require the aircraft to withstand impact forces of up to 175,000lb, based on a descent rate of 22.6fs. (US Navy)

79. In 1983 VS-30 celebrated its 30th Anniversary, and these markings were applied to the tail of the Air Group Commander's aircraft. The squadron was first formed with Grumman AF Guardians. (D. F. Brown)

80. Gear down, hook down and MAD boom extended, an S-3A assigned to the newly formed VS Support Unit based at NAS Jacksonville approaches its home base. Formed in 1984, the VS Support Unit conducts East Coast aircrew training similar to that of VS-41, the Viking training squadron at NAS North Island in southern California. (Author)

▲78   ▼79

80▲

▲81

81. Water vapour corkscrews off the propellers and steam rises from the catapult as an E-2C of VAW-125 launches from *John F. Kennedy*. The E-2C utilizes the same airframe as the earlier model of the Hawkeye, the E-2A, but it is fitted with improved long-range search radar and a carrier airborne inertial navigation system that will give the aircraft continued service life into the next decade. The first of the new E-2C Hawkeyes entered service in 1973. (K. Harrison/*Naval Aviation News*)

82. An E-2B serving with US Navy Reserve squadron VAW-88 taxies with wings folded during a 1982 training exercise at NAS Fallon, Nevada. All E-2A Hawkeyes have now been retrofitted in the field with improved avionics, receiving the designation E-2B. Grumman's E-2 Hawkeye was developed to replace another Grumman AEW aircraft, the E-1 Tracer, which itself was developed

▼82

from the S-2 Tracker. (Author)

83. Marine ground crew servicing an EA-6B Prowler of VMAQ-2. Derived from the original A-6 Intruder for electronic counter-measures duties, the new EA-6B was placed in production a year before the A-6E, and deliveries began in 1970. All EA-6As have now been replaced in front-line fleet squadrons and consigned to serve with Navy and Marine Rerserve units. (Phillip Huston)

84. The low-visibility grey camouflage on this A-6E from VMAT(AW)-202 shows how difficult it is to see and identify Navy and Marine aircraft painted in these drab, flat colours – and the aircraft is even more difficult to make out when at sea. A typical Carrier Air Wing will deploy ten squadrons of aircraft, one of which will comprise ten A-6 Intruders and four KA-6D tankers. (Author)

▲85 ▼86

87▲

85. The fourth production McDonnell Douglas AV-8B Harrier II, wearing low visibility camouflage, was evaluated at NAS Patuxent River in 1983. This paint scheme has not been adopted by the Marines since it is not practical for Harriers, and the standard British-style green and grey will continue on production AV-8Bs. (Author)

86. A Lockheed-built US-3 COD variant of the Viking serving with VRC-50 prepares to launch from USS *Enterprise* (CVN-65) during July 1983. The COD version carries a crew of five and a mixed load of six passengers and 4,600lb of cargo, or an all-cargo load of 7,500lb. Each of the two underwing cargo pods has a capacity of 1,000lb. (Tom Chee)

87. A P-3 assigned to VXN-8 at NAS Patuxent River and used as a training aircraft for the crews allocated to the Naval Oceanographic Office. Oceanographic Development Squadron VXN-8's sole responsibility is airborne oceanographic and geomagnetic research, and its fleet of three aircraft are assigned to Projects 'Magnet', 'Birdseye' and 'Seascan'. (Author)

88. A VQ-1 EA-3 Skywarrior seen aboard USS *Kitty Hawk* during a 1983 West Pacific cruise. More than twenty-five years of service attrition have taken their toll on the Skywarrior, and only a few remain in active service, mainly with electronic countermeasures squadrons. At one time the A-3 was the heaviest carrier-borne aircraft on the Navy's inventory. (Tom Chee)

88▼

▲89
89. An SH-2F Seasprite from HSL-34 shown during its week-long deployment aboard HMS *Hermes* during May 1983. HSL-34 joined *Hermes* following the ship's visit to Jacksonville, Florida, after returning from postwar service around the Falklands. From Jacksonville, *Hermes* sailed to Norfolk, her 800 Sqn. Sea Harriers flying off to NAS Oceana for joint USN/Royal Navy exercises. (Author)
▼90

90. The long-nosed OV-10D Broncos are modified OV-10As equipped with infra-red sensors and a Gatling gun mounted under the cockpit, the primary mission for this new version being night observation and strike. Several Broncos are reportedly being used to help track drug smugglers bringing cocaine into the United States from Colombia by sea or by air, thus providing realistic training for their crews. (Author)

91▲

92▲

91. Ground crew stand by during a VAW-126 E-2C engine run-up on the old seaplane ramp at NAS Norfolk. During carrier operations, E-2 aircraft are used to interface via data-link with F-14 Tomcats in order to extend the fleet air defence perimeter to 500 nautical miles. The E-2 can control up to three fighter squadrons with its two-way data-link, whilst its radar can detect and track as many as 300 targets and keep a file in its computer on the course, altitude and speed of each. (Author)

92. A P-3C Orion of VP-30 serving with Patrol Wing 1 (based at NAS Jacksonville) returns from patrol with its port outboard propeller feathered. The Lockheed P-3 is the US Navy's primary land-based ASW aircraft, introduced in 1960 as a replacement for the ageing P2V

Neptune. The Orion is derived from Lockheed's successful L-188 Electra turboprop civil airliner/cargo aircraft of the early 1950s. (US Navy)

93. A P-3B of Navy Reserve squadron VP-94. Based at NAS New Orleans, this unit was one of the last patrol squadrons to convert from SP-2H Neptunes during the mid-1970s. The Orion is fully equipped for its ASW role with extensive electronics in the fuselage, plus stowage for search stores and a 13ft-long bomb bay to accommodate torpedoes, depth bombs, mines or nuclear weapons; ten external underwing pylons can carry mines or rockets, and a searchlight is located under the starboard wing. (Author)

93▼

▲94

94. Another Navy Reserve patrol squadron is VP-68, which is based at NAS Patuxent River and whose aircraft and crews routinely fly the infamous 'Bermuda Triangle'. Reserve squadrons make up more than 30 per cent of the Navy's P-3 patrol units, and several are still equipped with the older P-3A and P-3B, although these are gradually being replaced by the newer P-3C. (Author)

95. A P-3A of VP-92, the Minuteman on its tail reflecting its NAS South Weymouth, Boston, home. The first pre-production P-3A flew on 15 April 1961 and, following flight-testing, evaluation and acceptance trials, deliveries to operational units began on 13 August 1963, VP-8 and VP-44 being the first squadrons to receive the type.

P-3Bs were put into production during 1965, introducing many improvements in ASW equipment which included a new ECM direction-finder. (Author)

96. RP-3 'Arctic Fox' was assigned to Project 'Birdseye' for ice reconnaissance and ice research by the Naval Oceanographic Office; 'Arctic Fox', along with 'El Coyote' and 'Roadrunner', are all part of Oceanographic Development Squadron VXN-8, a Fleet unit under the Commander-in-Chief US Atlantic Fleet. The squadron functions as a distinct entity but receives technical direction from the Naval Oceanographic Office and the Defense Mapping Agency. (Author)

97. A rare example of the VP-3A Orion, which is used as a VIP transport for the Chief of Naval Operations and is operated by VP-30. The VP-3A is fitted with air-liner-style seats in place of the usual array of radar screens and consoles normally associated with Orions, and is often found flying VIPs and high ranking military officers to some of the Navy's more remote bases. Note the absence of a MAD boom. (Author)

97 ▶

◄98

98. A P-3A of VP-66, one of twelve Navy Reserve P-3 squadrons, on final approach to its home station at NAS Willow Grove. The red Liberty Bell on the tailfin is surrounded by thirteen blue stars, representing the thirteen original American colonies. P-3As were handed down to the Reserves from regular Navy units as newer P-3C and P-3C Update Orions entered service; these older P-3s still have a lot of useful service left, and help fill the Navy's need for operational patrol aircraft. (Author)

▲99

99. In active service since 1952, the Douglas C-118 Liftmaster now serves with just two units, VR-52 at NAS Willow Grove (an aircraft from this base is seen here just after take-off) and VR-54 at NAS Atlanta. Douglas C-9s will replace the six remaining C-118s by 1986. Sixty-four C-118s – military versions of the Douglas DC-6 civil airliner – were ordered for the US Navy, originally serving as the Navy's contribution to the Military Air Transport Service (MATS). (Author)

100. The original Grumman C-1A Trader, pictured here, is still serving after more than thirty years, having survived three belly landings and a 1978 fire aboard USS *Forrestal*. A total of 87 C-1A Traders, first designated TF-1s, were produced by Grumman; perhaps only forty of these remain in active Navy service today, new Grumman-built C-2 Greyhounds replacing them in the COD mission.

▼100

101. Wings fold on a C-1A following a landing on board USS *Lexington.* COD C-1A Traders deliver mail, spare parts and personnel to aircraft carriers at sea. Derived from the Grumman S-2 Tracker, the C-1A is the last of the Trader/Tracker/Tracer series built by Grumman: the S-2 Tracker has been replaced by Lockheed's S-3 Viking and the E-1 Tracer by Grumman's E-2 Hawkeye, but the C-1A is expected to serve beyond 1990, giving it nearly forty years of continuous service. (Author)

102. UC-12As are operated as utility and liaison aircraft by most Navy and Marine Corps air stations, replacing the older C-117s, C-54s and US-2s that have now all been retired from active service. The UC-12 is the military version of the Beech King Air and is equipped with the most up-to-date pilot and navigation aids. Its excellent flying characteristics and ease of maintenance make it an ideal aircraft for its role. (Author)

▲103 ▼104

105▲

103. A Lockheed KC-130R tanker/transport operated by US Marine Corps squadron VMRG-252 taking off from Goose Bay, Labrador, in 1982; the -R is an updated version of the original KC-130F (formerly designated GV-1), first delivered to the Marines in 1960. Several squadrons of USMC KC-130s were staging through Goose Bay on this day on their way home following the completion of a NATO exercise. (Author)

104. A US Navy ski-equipped LC-130F Hercules serving with VXE-6 during May 1983. The brightly painted LC-130Fs are used to resupply Navy research stations in the Antarctic. In 1960 four such aircraft fitted with skis and other modifications for Antarctic service were ordered by the Navy and were originally designated C-130BL. (Don Spering/AIR)

105. An OV-10A Bronco of Marine Corps Reserve squadron VMO-4. The new long-nosed OV-10D is now replacing the A-models serving with the Marines. The OV-10 was first developed and tested as an Army, Navy and Air Force project, but the original specifications were drawn up by the USMC as a Light Armed Reconnaissance Airplane. Broncos saw extensive service in Vietnam as forward air controllers (FACs) and in counter-insurgency (COIN) operations. (Author)

106. A North-American T-2C Buckeye all-purpose jet trainer of Navy training squadron VT-23. More than 450 Buckeyes of all variants have been produced since 1958, many entering service with foreign air forces. The first flight of the T-2A, originally designated T2J-1, took place on 7 February 1958 at North American's Columbus, Ohio, facility. Buckeyes were first delivered to the Navy Training Command at NAS Pensacola, and later to NAS Meridan and training squadrons VT-7 and VT-9. (Author)

106▼

▲107

108▲

107. A TA-3B Skywarrior of VAQ-33 lands aboard *Carl Vinson*. In addition to its fleet ECM duties, VAQ-33 is also responsible for Skywarrior aircrew training for the Navy. Although long overdue for replacement, Douglas Skywarriors are still serving in small numbers, primarily with VAQ-33, based at NAS Key West, in the electronic intelligence role for the various Carrier Air Wings. Only twelve TA-3Bs (originally designated A3D-2Ts) were produced, in the early 1960s, the aircraft being equipped with a pressurized fuselage and accommodation for six radar/navigation pupils, an instructor and a pilot. (Author)
108. Affectionately referred to as 'The Whale' by its aircrews, the KA-3B tanker variant of the Skywarrior now serves with only two Navy Reserve squadrons, VAK-208 and VAK-308. Beginning in 1957, approximately fifty A-3B Skywarriors were produced by Douglas with design provision for a weapons bay that not only could carry a wide range of stores but could also be fitted with a flight refuelling pack which incorporated a 1,082 Imp. gallon fuel tank. When the A-3B became obsolete as a front-line attack aircraft it was converted to the tanker version, taking full advantage of its remaining years in service. (Tom Chee)
109. This rather unusual and radical modification of the Skywarrior is designated NRA-3B and was serving with the Pacific Missile Test Center in 1982 as a special airborne test platform. This is perhaps the last modification the Skywarrior will receive as the aircraft's service life is not expected to be extended beyond 1990. (Author)

109▼

110. Powered by two General Electric J85 engines, the Buckeye has been the Navy's primary jet trainer for almost 25 years, its student pilots graduating to high-performance fighters such as the F-4, F-14 and the new F-18. Navy and Marine pilots selected for jet basic training graduate to T-2Cs after completing the 35-hour primary course in Beech T-34Cs. The T-2C variant made its first flight on 17 April 1968. (Author)

◀111   112▲   113▼

111. More familiar in USAF markings is Northrop's T-38 Talon. Several T-38s are operational with VF-43 at NAS Oceana as 'Aggressors' for air combat training, and at 'Top Gun', the US Navy's graduate fighter pilot school. VF-43's T-38s are actually used as adversary instructors' training aircraft and for occasional air combat engagements, and the machines are on loan from the Air Force until new F-5Fs can replace them. (William Cline/USN)

112. In addition to T-38s, Northrop F-5E Tigers are assigned to VF-43, an example being seen here returning to NAS Oceana following an air combat training exercise with F-14 Tomcats. VF-43 is a dual-mission squadron: first, it provides all-weather instrument training and flight training to Atlantic Fleet pilots and replacement pilots; and second, it provides air combat adversary services to Atlantic Fleet fighter and attack squadrons, as well as to Marine and Air Force units. (Author)

113. The US Navy Test Pilot School at NAS Patuxent River utilizes five T-38s for specialized test pilot training. (Author)

▲114

114. Possibly the only remaining De Havilland U-6A Beaver left in US military service is on strength with the US Navy Test Pilot School; more remarkable still is the fact that this former US Army aircraft, acquired during the 1960s, is the first, and perhaps the only, Beaver operated by the US Navy. (Author)

115. British Aerospace Hawks built under licence by McDonnell Douglas are expected to enter US Navy service as primary jet trainers by the late 1980s. In January 1980 the two companies joined together to propose a carrier-suitable version of the Hawk to fulfil the US Navy's VTXTS requirements. The aircraft is seen as a replacement for both the T-2C Buckeye and the TA-4J Skyhawk. (British Aerospace)

116. Kaman SH-2F Seasprites serve in the anti-submarine search and strike role aboard Navy destroyers and frigates. Referred to as

LAMPS (Light Airborne Multi-Purpose System), Seasprite entered service as a single-engined utility/search and rescue helicopter on 18 December 1962. During the Vietnam War newer twin-engined Seasprites, armed with machine guns in a chin turret, served in combat search and rescue missions in the Gulf of Tonkin. (Author)

117. A pair of SH-2F Seasprites from training squadron HSL-30 leave NAS Norfolk. During December 1971 the LAMPS-equipped Seasprites became operational, adding to both the defensive and the offensive capabilities of US Navy destroyers operating in anti-submarine duties and providing for the first time effective 'over-the-horizon' and 'beyond-radar' search and strike systems. HSL-30 is responsible for training both new Seasprite pilots and maintenance personnel. (Author)

▼115

▲118 ▼119

118. A Sikorsky SH-60B Seahawk during a 1982 test flight. Seahawks equipped with LAMPS III weapons systems will replace SH-2F Seasprites in the ASW role by the end of the decade. On 24 March 1983 the first production SH-60B, from the first production batch of eighteen helicopters, was delivered to the US Navy; in total, 204 Seahawks are on order by the Navy, with deliveries continuing through the 1980s. The first SH-60B Seahawk squadron, HSL-41 at NAS North Island, was formed during the summer of 1984, a second squadron following at NAS Jacksonville. (Sikorsky)

119. Sikorsky SH-3H Sea Kings provide anti-submarine search duties from aboard aircraft carriers, in addition to search and rescue duties. A Sea King of HS-9 'Sea Griffins' prepares for an SAR flight from *Nimitz* during the summer of 1982. Sikorsky's Sea King gained great prominence during the 1960s when the helicopters were routinely watched by millions of people when used for the recovery of America's astronauts from their space capsules following their return from earth orbit and splashdown – a slightly different role from that which the Sea King was designed to perform! (D. F. Brown)

120. Four Navy Reserve squadrons operate such Sea Kings as this SH-3G (of HS-75), shown landing at NAS Willow Grove and wearing the standard scheme of grey and white, with the squadron's green/yellow/green fuselage stripes. Helicopters like the Sea King are ideal for the anti-submarine role, thanks to their ability to hover over the sea and listen for underwater objects with dipping sonar. The Sea King made its first flight on 11 March 1959 and will continue to serve through to the end of the decade and beyond. (Author)

▼121 ▲122

121. The new three-engined CH-53E Super Sea Stallion, seen here serving with HM-12 at NAS Norfolk, entered service in 1983 and provided the Navy and Marine Corps with a much-desired increase in lift capability. The prototype Super Sea Stallion, designated YCH-53E, was first flown on 1 March 1974 at Sikorsky's Stratford plant. The CH-53E is a 'growth' design based on the CH-53D currently in service with the Navy and Marines, and offers increased performance and capability over the previous variants. (Author)

122. A close-up view of the long-range fuel tanks of a CH-53E reveals a new Navy term, 'VOD Det' – a reference to Vertical On-board Delivery Detachment. (Author)

▲123 ▼124

125▲

123. Sea Stallion squadron HM-16, operating the RH-53D minesweeping variant, was formed in 1982; in the same year the unit participated in the multi-national Suez Canal minesweeping operation. HM-16 also took part in Operation 'Blue Light', sending eight of its Sea Stallions to help in that ill-fated mission to rescue American hostages held in Iran. (Author)

124. Marine Corps Reserve squadrons also operate CH-53As in small numbers, as illustrated by this Sea Stallion of HMH-772 landing at its home station, NAS Willow Grove; Marine Reserve squadrons come under the command of Marine Air Wing 4. The first CH-53A prototype made its maiden flight on 14 October 1964, at which time it was the largest and heaviest helicopter produced outside the Soviet Union. (Author)

125. The Boeing Vertol CH-46 Sea Knight is jointly operated by the Navy and Marines. Here a Navy CH-46D from the Navy supply ship *Savannah* delivers a sling load of cargo to the flight deck of an LPH. Official acceptance trials of the CH-46A were completed by November 1964, just over two years from the date of its first flight, and by the summer of 1965 five Marine Corps squadrons were operating the new helicopters. (Boeing Vertol)

126. A Marine Corps CH-46D hovers and its crew chief stands at the cabin door observing the sway of his sling load. During 1964 the US Navy purchased slightly modified Sea Knights for replenishment operations between combat supply ships and combatant vessels at sea, the first UH-46A being delivered to US Navy helicopter utility squadron VHU-1 during July that year. (Author)

126▼

▲127

127. Both the Navy and Marines employ Sea Knights, some with high visibility red markings, in search and rescue duties from air stations; pictured is a CH-46A taking off for SAR duties at MCAS Beaufort. A total of 624 CH-46 Sea Knights were delivered to the US Navy and Marine Corps between 1964 and 1971, and in 1980 Boeing Vertol was awarded a $24.7 million contract for a multi-year improvement programme to upgrade Sea Knights to CH-46E standards, thus extending the helicopter's effective service life beyond the 1990s. (Author)

128. AH-1J SeaCobras serve only with Marine and Marine Reserve units; a SeaCobra of one such unit, HMA-773 of the Marine Reserve, is seen here hovering on the Marine flight line at NAS Atlanta prior to a pilot check ride (the instructor taking the front gunner's seat). Developed specifically for the Marine Crops, the AH-1J differs from its US Army counterpart in having twin Pratt & Whitney T400 turbine engines as opposed to the Army Cobra's single engine. Iran and the Spanish Navy also operate Bell's SeaCobra. (Author)

▼128